Soul of a Diva

of a

A Memoir in Verse

COSMIC GIRL

iUniverse

SOUL OF A DIVA
A MEMOIR IN VERSE

iUniverse books may be ordered through booksellers or by contacting:

iUniverse
1663 Liberty Drive
Bloomington, IN 47403
www.iuniverse.com
1-800-Authors (1-800-288-4677)

Because of the dynamic nature of the internet, any web addresses or links contained in this book may have changed since publication and may no longer be valid. The views expressed in this work are solely those of the author and do not necessarily reflect the views of the publisher, and the publisher hereby disclaims any responsibility for them.

Any people depicted in stock imagery provided by Getty Images are models, and such images are being used for illustrative purposes only.
Certain stock imagery © Getty Images.

ISBN: 978-1-5320-8453-9 (sc)
ISBN: 978-1-5320-8454-6 (e)

Library of Congress Control Number: 2019915945

Print information available on the last page.

iUniverse rev. date: 10/22/2019

THIS BOOK IS DEDICATED TO ALL THOSE WHO HAVE LOVED AND LOST, THOSE WHO ARE LOOKING FOR LOVE EVERLASTING, AND ESPECIALLY THE LUCKY ONES WHO HAVE FOUND LOVE ETERNAL.

Acknowledgments

I would like to give a special thanks to those especially close to me who have stood by me through it all. Thank you for being there to help me fight my battles, for giving me the strength and love to face challenges head-on, and for encouraging me to go for it, heart and soul! And thanks to all those who have helped to inspire me and to make this book a reality.

Stay strong!

Stay beautiful!

Stay fierce!

About the Book

So what is a diva? *Merriam-Webster* defines a diva as a famous female opera singer, a self-important person who is temperamental and difficult to please. According to the *Urban Dictionary*, a diva is a fierce, often temperamental singer who "comes correct." She does not "sweat the haters." As for me, I'd like to use another definition for a diva: one who exudes great style and personality with confidence, expresses her own style, and doesn't let others influence who she is or who she wants to be—fierce!

This book is a reflection of experiences, relationships, heartbreaks, and inspirations. A lot of us find ourselves in situations that make us feel as if we are the only one going through it and that no one else could possibly understand.

Soul of a Diva envelops the feelings and emotions of the heart by viewing societal woes and dreaming of lost loves, passionate encounters, and unconditional love. This journey focuses on those issues surrounding us, things in society and throughout the world that happen to affect us. These poems take a sensual approach and tug close to the heart, reaching deep and delving into the unconditional, all-consuming emotions that love can bring about.

I hope these poems touch you in some way. Continue to share your heart with those close to you, cultivate and cherish the friendships you have, and remember that family is where the heart is.

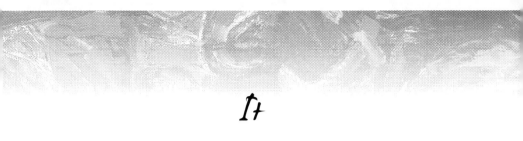

It

Can you feel it?
This force that was put into motion
When we were born.

The closer we get,
The more it's magnified,
And no matter how much we try to fight it,
No matter how much we try to ignore it,
That force will always be there,
Pulling us together.

Since the dawn of time,
We were meant to be together.
It's a force greater
Than the both of us.

There's no use fighting it anymore.

Summer's (Southern) Love

Hot summer nights under a full moon,
Neptune's Monsoons at the Port of Call,
Whiskey sour pool parties,
And you.

Frozen daiquiris and late-night strolls
Through the Quarter,
Drinking rainbows under the
Flaming fountain,
Skinny-dipping and making love
Under the diving board.

That summer you showed me so many things.
There has never been another time
When I felt so free,
So uninhibited, and so in love
All at the same time.

You were the first to teach me
How to drive a stick,
How to tie a cherry stem into a knot
With my tongue (ha ha!),
And the "art" of drinking vodka straight.

You.
No one else has truly understood that in order to love me,
You must accept me for who I am and not change me.
Only you. You loved me with all my faults and insane quirks.
I love you, my summer's southern love.

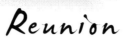

Reunion

It's been twenty years since we've gazed into each other's eyes,
When summers lasted forever and
Nights never ended.
When I saw you that night at the wedding,
All those memories came back like
It was yesterday.
Gazing into your eyes,
Feeling your arms around my waist,
Seeing that smile of yours,
There was so much I wanted to say.

And now we are going to be reunited after
So many years.
Will it be like old times?
How much can I expect
Now that we are back in each other's lives?
It's funny, but even after all this time,
My feelings are just as strong as ever.
I hope this feeling never ends.

Soul Mates

When love transcends through space and time,
When two can communicate the same thoughts
Without saying a word,
When they can accept each other unconditionally
And love each other endlessly as if
They are the same,
Body and soul,
Nothing can break that bond.

When there is a trust so deep that it's
Beyond explanation,
When a simple picture from past times can mean so much,
When the passage of time—even without contact and despite social
distractions—only serves to strengthen their bond,
No one can touch that feeling.

It's a bond that can't be broken,
A love that's beyond space and time,
A connection like no other:
Soul mates.

Thoughts of You

Endless gazes into your deep, dark eyes
That speak no words yet say so much.
Countless daydreams of times shared,
Talking, laughing, loving.

Growing up, we spent endless nights
Strolling through cobblestone streets.
Now I spend endless hours
Longing to be wrapped in your arms.

Your smile, your touch, your kiss, your eyes—
All these things and more
Draw me deeper into you
With each passing day.

Tears of Passion

When love overflows and can't be contained,
When the passion touches you so deep
And so hard that you feel as if you'll explode,

When the love you feel for that person is
Bigger than yourself—
So big it's as if you're drowning in a
Sea of emotion—
You realize how powerful love can be.

And it comes with the power to overcome
Any obstacle, any barrier,
And conquer all for the sake of love.

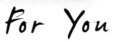

For You

I love you
With all my heart,
Completely and unconditionally,
Unyielding and endlessly.

So I give this to you
To hold close in times of frustration
Or doubt, or anytime you need a friend.
Whenever you just feel like reminiscing over old times
Or are thinking about our next chance encounter,
Just promise to cherish it and handle it with care,

And it will be there for you always.

You

You came back into my life,
And it was like magic;
Every moment with you is so perfect,
So wonderful.
The way we think the same things
And feel the same way,
It's incredible.

For so long I've always felt alone in this world,
Like there was no one in this world
I could really trust, really open up to.
But now for the first time I finally feel
Close to someone.
With you I know that no matter what happens,
Everything will be okay.

You are the most amazing man I have
Ever known,
A true godsend.
I am so thankful that fate has given us
Another chance.
This time, I won't take anything for granted.

My Eternal Flame

You are my heart and soul,
My entire being,
My knight in shining armor,
My guardian angel.

You are my strength,
My inspiration,
My touchstone,
My soul mate,
My other half.

You are the sun,
The moon, the stars.
You are everything to me.
You are my eternal flame.

The Mighty Lion

Behold the mighty lion!
Fierce and majestic,
Yet gentle and nurturing.
He is one who will give his all for those close to him
And strike fear into the hearts of those
Who cross him.

Being no stranger to adversity,
The mighty lion pulls strength from
These life lessons
To guide others with his wisdom.

Look into the eyes of the lion and you'll see
A passion that runs deep into his soul.
It is expressed through his warm caresses,
His sweet, soft kisses,
And the way he ravages his lover,
Conquering her for his own.

Behold the mighty lion!
Strong. Passionate. Peaceful.
Standing regal as he gazes
Upon earth's unbeaten paths.

Incredible

Your eyes
Behold the wisdom of a thousand pharaohs.

Your mouth
Beautiful, distinctive, seductive.

Your hands
Give strength and tenderness
With each warm caress.

Every glance, every touch, every kiss, every stroke,
Every moment with you is

Incredible.

Stray Thoughts

Fingers stroking skin,
Making toes curl,
Sending chills through my body,
Making me want more.

Tongues in the heat of passion.
Juices flowing.
Skin tingling with desire,
Wanting you now.

I want to feel you,
Your body pressed against mine,
Your touch, your caress.
I want to feel your eyes piercing my soul.

I want to feel your mouth
As it explores every inch of my skin,
Enveloping me entirely,
Taking all of me in.

Take me!
Ravage me!
Go deep inside me.
Make me scream in ecstasy!
Take me! Make me *yours*,
All yours,
Until I scream no more.

The Cheaters

It all started one snow-stormy weekend;
We were hanging out just as friends.
Then we got stranded together,
And so it began.

You knew I was involved with someone else,
But the company was nice,
So we agreed that things would be cool,
Just some fun with a little added spice!

But as time went on,
Something started happening.
I saw how nurturing you were,
How well we blended with each other's kids,
The little things you'd do to make me smile,
And the passion that ran deeper and deeper
Each time we made love.

Five Days

Your eyes, so impactful.
Your skin, so soft, so responsive.
Your touch, so passionate.

Waking up to your touch, your embrace,
Feeling your skin against mine.

With no inhibitions,
You made love to me like no man
Has ever done before,
Exploring every inch of me,
Leaving your indelible mark on my soul.

You gave me so much
During our brief time together,
More than I could ever express.

Thank you for the most amazing, exciting,
Erotic, beautiful, passionate,
Unforgettable moment of my life.

Home

After so many years
I finally realized
That one of the most romantic moments
In my life
Is falling asleep in your arms.
Not hearing from you for two weeks
Feels like a lifetime.

After so many years
I finally realized
Just being with you washes all my stress away
And why, of all the people in the world,
You're the only one I trust with my life.

Because you're home to me.

You're that safe place I can go to
When the rest of the world seems so scary.
You're that solid foundation
When all else seems so uncertain.
Your smile, your eyes,
The soothing sound of your voice,
All that and more remind me
That when I am with you,
I am home.

Lost in Limbo

I tried to move on,
To forget about the past,
But I just couldn't move past it.
I'm lost in limbo.

You told me you'd be there for me,
And then you just disappeared,
After all that we've been through,
After all that we've shared …

So I try to move on
And forget about the past,
But just when I think I'm over you,
I'm lost in limbo.

I just wanted an explanation,
Just a reason for what happened,
Something, anything, that could keep me
From being lost in limbo.

But you still refuse.
After all the trials,
I never thought it would be you
Who would have me

Lost in limbo.

Highway of Life

On the highway of life
You're moving a hundred miles an hour,
And I'm just trying to thumb a ride.

Your career—your life—has many demands,
And I want to be there,
To stand by you and support you,
But will I be sacrificing my inner self?
Will you be there for me when I need you?
Are you ready to take me into
Your life completely?
To build a family together?
Or will I be left alone,
Waiting for you in the dark?

Our love has taken us on an incredible journey,
Yet the journey has just begun.

Used Up

When I'm going down the street
Just trying to get to work,
And I hear, "Hey, baby, how you doin'?"
I feel all used up.

When I go out to the club with someone,
Trying to have a few drinks and some fun,
And all he wants is one thing,
I feel all used up.

When things continuously pile up,
One thing after another, after another,
And it seems like there's just no way out,
I feel all used up.

I need to break away!
I need to escape!
I need to go somewhere
To replenish my soul
Before it gets
All used up.

One Wish

They say when you wish upon a star,
All your wishes will come true,
But for so many years now,
My only wish has been to be with you.

You have always been the one
Who truly sees me, deep into my soul;
Your strength and understanding
Serve as the foundation of our undying love.

You mean so much more to me
Than any words can say.

First Time

Games of jailbreak,
Tackling each other and
Ripping T-shirts to shreds.
Sharing a first kiss.

Years go by,
And feelings are stronger than ever.
Stealing moments alone,
We make out behind the house.

Years go by still.
We reminisce of days past.
Still our hearts beat as one.
That night we made love
For the very first time.
It was amazing.

You were my first love at twelve
And my truest love throughout life.
You wrote me my first poem
And gave me my first kiss.

We have had a lot of firsts:
First kiss, first love,
And a bond that has withstood the test of time.

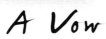

A Vow

Looking back to when we first met,
I see there was that instant spark of attraction,

Being immediately drawn to each other
As if guided by some higher power.

As we spent time together,
I found that I trusted you completely,
Even though we had only just met.

Now, after so many years of being apart,
That spark has ignited into a flame
(An eternal flame).
There is no one in this world
I trust more than you.
I trust you with my life.

Your mere presence
Washes all my stress away instantaneously,
Giving me a sense of peace and renewed strength
That can be found nowhere else.

You are everything to me.
You're the first person I think of
When I wake up in the morning
And the last person I think of
When I go to sleep at night.

You complete me.
And so I promise
To do whatever is in my power
To please you and make you happy
For the rest of eternity.

Your Love Is Real

Your love is real,
Raw,
Pure,
Natural, and untainted.

It is all-consuming,
Enveloping my heart and devouring my soul.

With you I know there is no hesitation,
No question, and no doubt.

As our souls intermingle,
Our passion takes us to unimaginable, animalistic heights.

Never had I imagined that something or someone
So amazing, so beautiful,
Could be so real.

Every moment of every day,
I thank the heavens
For the gift that is you.

Make It Stop

The feeling,
The emotion,
The pain,
Make it stop.
Since you've been gone,
There's this emptiness that can't be filled.

You said to never change,
To stay warm and passionate and caring.

But to stop the feeling,
To stop the emotion,
To stop the pain,
To stop the emptiness,
I will have to turn my heart cold
Until you come to warm my soul again.

Damaged

Throughout life
We stumble upon events
That leave an indelible mark
On our souls.

In Your Arms

If I think hard enough,
I can still feel myself being wrapped
In your arms,
Your warm embrace,
Your loving caress.

You sang "No Ordinary Love."
We drank by the flaming fountain.
You spoke of us getting married,
And we secretly hoped the night
Would never end.

Endless talks about everything and nothing.
The songs "Pink Cashmere" and "Purple Rain"
Playing in the background.
Time seemed to stand still
If only for a brief moment …

There is no place I'd rather be
At any moment, at any time,
Than wrapped sweetly, lovingly,
And forever in your arms.

At the Dinner Table

As I sit at the table
Beautifully set with fine china and crystal,
I think back to when I was a girl of twelve,
And I recall the loving advice of my aunt:
"Young ladies always eat
With only one hand on the table."

Before and since then,
My aunt has served
As the matriarch of the family.
Serving as friend, mother, aunt,
And grandmother,
She has been there to give advice
On relationships, health issues, dating, etiquette—
Almost anything you could imagine.

And now that we have all grown older
And hopefully a little wiser,
The occasion comes every now and then
When she may even ask one of us for advice.
My aunt mama,
Always there for love, guidance, support,
A home-cooked meal, a warm embrace,
I love you always.

Black Heart

He says,
"I love you so much.
I'll always be there for you.
I will never hurt you.
I'm not going anywhere."
And then he's gone …

And instead of Afua Cooper asking,
"When soul and soul kiss,
Who can stop the love?"
You stare in the mirror asking,
"When heart and heart meet,
Who can stop the pain?"

That pain that reaches
Into the depths of your soul
And rips out your heart.

But no more.
No more pain.
No more love.
Your heart has turned black
Like the hole he left in your soul,
Never to feel again.

Sugar Daddy

I know your type,
Always so generous, so giving,
Pretending to understand
My every need.

You're always there when I call,
Speaking words of encouragement,
But that's just you trying to get in my head,
Trying to manipulate and control.

Now I'm taking back control!
I don't need your gifts, your services.
I am a strong, independent woman,
And I refuse to be anyone's
Little "sugar" on the side!

So keep on steppin', Daddy,
'Cause this sugar ain't buying it!

Desert Son

You are beautiful.
Your skin,
A deep golden reflection of your desert home.
Your eyes,
Reflecting the battles of your ancestors past.
Your compassion,
Wanting to find a cure for all that
Ails the world.

Your smile is like the sun,
Bringing warmth and joy to all those
Around you,
Your gentle spirit
Lending others strength and wisdom.

Like the rulers and kings before you,
You stand regal,
Protecting those close to you
From danger in times of adversity.

Desert son,
A gift from the gods for all to behold!

The Squeeze Test

It starts with a gentle stroke up the back,
Slowly rubbing up and down,
Touching me deeply yet gently
As I close my eyes in anticipation of more.

As you come around toward my front,
Your hand glides down my side.
Gazing deep into my eyes,
You reach down,
Grabbing handfuls of flesh to fill your urge.

Then finally your kiss envelops me.
Your arms take all of me in
As I stretch up on my tippy-toes,
Wanting for more.

Did I pass the squeeze test?
Maybe you need to give me one more squeeze
Just to make sure.
Ready?

Don't Tell

At six years old,
One day I got lost taking a new way
Home from school.
A nice police officer drove me home.
What would he say if I gathered up the courage
To tell him what happens
When I go home every day?

Would he believe me if I told him
Of the numerous parties that occurred
Where everyone drank to excess
From noon 'til night, including me?

What would he say if I told him of the drugs—
Marijuana, coke, pills—that were sold and used
Regularly, on a daily basis, around the house?

One day my family gave me a joint to smoke.
They thought it would be "cool"
To see li'l sis get high.

Another day I was in the house
Alone with my sister's boyfriend.
He started kissing my leg and grabbing me.
"*Stop!*" I told him. "*Let me go!*"
And I ran away.
Just another victim.

They always said, "Don't tell
'Cause no one will believe you anyway."
So I just got out of Officer Friendly's car
And smiled and waved as he dropped
Me off at home,
Ready for another day of battle.

For What?

You say you still love me;
What am I supposed to do with that?
After the lonely nights,
The arguments,
The "misunderstandings,"
What is that supposed to mean?

It's been over between us,
And after all this time,
After moving on, going our separate ways,
You still love me.
For what?!

Huh, what?
'Cause I don't go backward;
I move forward.
And to go back with you
Just wouldn't make any sense.

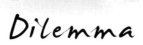

Dilemma

To be in love would be
So wonderful,
To have someone
To confide in, to rely on,
To give yourself to.

But to do that would mean
Getting hurt, being vulnerable, becoming damaged.
And I can't go through that again.

Dodging the Bullet

Every time our black men
In the prime of their youth
Step out the door,
They are dodging a bullet,

Fighting for their lives
To make it to the top,
To make it out of the 'hood,
To make it across the street
Without getting arrested, shot, killed—
Just dodging that bullet.

Every time we get on that
Metro train to our final destination,
Or cross the street,
Or lie down with a new lover,
We are just dodging a bullet.

You hear women on TV telling us
To become "one less"
When every day, every second,
There is one more with
HPV, AIDS,
A person who was just trying
To dodge that bullet.

People now who have diabetes,
Heart disease, cancer,
Fighting for one more year,
One more month, one more day,
To dodge that bullet.

So what do we do?
Do we keep running?
Or do we just give up hope?
Or do we *fight*?
Yeah, fight.

Superhero

The Caped Crusader,
The Man of Steel,
The Dark Knight.
These men are called superheroes,
Symbolic of those representing truth,
Justice, and honor.
But they aren't real. They don't exist.

The media only creates heroes
Such as these so that we have
A means of escape.
But we are forgetting that heroes,
Even superheroes, really do exist.

They are the countless people of color
Who sacrificed everything,
Even their lives,
So that the next generation
Could move that much closer
To equality.
These are our heroes.

And the many men and women,
Nearly children themselves,
Protecting our country in the armed forces,
Fighting for unknown causes,
Coming home to broken dreams
And broken lives;
These are our heroes.

And the mother, father, teacher,
Neighbor, friend—
That special someone in your life
Who is always there for you
To lift you up, be there for you,
Give you a shoulder to cry on,
And give you strength …

Heroes.

Saboteurs

We are so good together
And have so many good times,
But still I hold back.

An argument can start
Over the slightest thing,
Leaving you dazed and confused.

It's not you; it's him.
Like him, I've become a saboteur,
Avoiding a relationship,
Lashing out against those
Who claim to give their love.

It's no one's fault. It's reflex.
I'm unable to fight
The one who is truly to blame,
So I leave a trail of innocent victims
In my path.

Love

Love.
It makes the world go 'round.
It's a many-splendored thing;
It heals the world.
It's unconditional.
But

If it's magic,
Why does it hurt so much?
Why does it kill so slowly?
Why can't we make it everlasting?

Let's revive this precious commodity.
Stop the pain, the hurt, the killing.
Open your heart and your mind
To love *all* your neighbors
And make this world beautiful
For generations to come.

Warrior

Battle!

I am a child witness of rape,
A daughter of divorce,
The child of a mother who was more
A woman of cunning and resourcefulness
Than a nurturer.
I learned early on that
Absolute loyalty was key
To getting ahead.
And so I survived.

I am a single mother
Battling a crack-addicted baby daddy,
Trying to make ends meet,
Doing whatever I have to,
To make sure my son is safe,
To be sure he grows up as
A strong black man.
And so I fight.

I am a woman of passion.
I have felt the deepest heartbreak
And some of the greatest joys.
I have been kissed on the hand by a
(Former) KGB general.
I have mixed and mingled with
Celebrities and dignitaries alike,
And I have even given a cigar
To a United States president.
And so I write.

I may be war-torn,
At times weary,
But never weakening.

I *am* a warrior!

A Person of Value

I am the quiet little girl
Living in a house of drugs and alcohol,
Learning early on that
Inner strength is key to survival.
I am a person of value.

I am the fashion model
Who was always the new kid in school,
Never quite fitting in with the other kids,
Being teased, *bullied*, because
I am neither black nor white
But a mixture of worldly cultures.
Being pushed, shoved—
Always the outcast.
I am a person of value.

I am a single mother
Going to college to get her degree,
Working to make a better life
For myself and my son.
Fighting to keep my son out of jail
And off the streets,
Struggling through all of life's obstacles.
I am a person of value.

At times I felt doubtful,
Insecure, not "good enough."
But what does that mean?
At what point am I worth something
In other people's eyes?

All people are of value at the onset.
They are God's most precious gift.
So remember, no matter what anyone says,
You are a person of value.

I See You, Man

I see you, man,
Standing there on the threshold of adulthood,
Preparing yourself to face the world
And stand on your own.

It seemed like just yesterday
That you were taking your first steps,
Learning your first words,
And discovering all the new things around you.

You have always been one to stand up
To a challenge.
And when faced with a problem,
You were determined to work it out in
Your own way.

When real trouble came,
Your strong sense of determination and focus
Helped guide you through
With love and support from those around you.

Times weren't always easy for us,
But we always managed,
And although we sometimes fought,
There was always love.

I see you, man.
I mean I *really* see you.
From the small child you used to be
To the man you are today, I see you.
I am so proud of the man you are
And the man you have yet to become.
And I am so glad to have you as my son.

Shine

Outcast. Oddball.
Nerd. Weirdo.
These words are used
To label those who don't fit in,
Those who are to be excluded
From the popular ones,
The "beautiful" ones.

But it's these same things
That make us unique,
That make us beautiful,
Extraordinary, amazing!

Even the ugly duckling
Grew to be a beautiful swan.
And diamonds—synonymous with
Beauty, extravagance, and even royalty—
Are derived from coal.

So embrace your uniqueness!
Be different. Be extraordinary.
Be fabulous. *Be you!*

And don't ever let anyone
Take away your sparkle.

Printed in the United States
By Bookmasters